Knock-Knock Jokes and Silly Stories for Kids

Knock-Knock Jokes and Silly Stories for Kids

May B. Gigglin

FOREWORD BY
Toby Price

ILLUSTRATED BY
Jeremy Nguyen

A Brightly Book

Z Kids • New York

Published in the United States by Z Kids, an imprint of Zeitgeist™,
a division of Penguin Random House LLC, New York.
penguinrandomhouse.com

Zeitgeist™ is a trademark of Penguin Random House LLC

ISBN: 9780593436035
Ebook ISBN: 9780593435755

Illustrations by Jeremy Nguyen
Cover design by Erin Yeung
Interior design by Emma Hall

Edited by Erin Nelson

Printed in the United States of America

3rd Printing

First Edition

A Note from Principal Butts

One of my earliest memories was in a gas station in Ohio. My dad, about to pay for gas, saw me spinning a rack of comic books, a growing stack in my hands. He motioned for me to bring the books over. To my great surprise, he bought all of them on the spot.

The secret my dad knew was that if I was going to become a big reader, I needed to practice. If I was going to practice, I needed books I *actually* wanted to read. From that day on, Dad helped fill my room with comic books, choose-your-own-adventure books, joke books, even elaborate pop-up books. You see, each of those books had something in common. They taught me reading was fun. In fact, reading became something I wanted to do all the time.

When it came time to set my own kids on their reading journey, my wife and I made sure silly, high-interest books were at the top of the list. As a parent of two kids with autism, I believe silly books are not only fun, they are also an essential tool to foster communication.

No matter who you are or what your story is, there is room for more silly—more jokes that make us giggle and stories about farts. Because when kids engage with books that tickle them down to their funny bone, they not only have a good time, silly-story gigglers become readers for life.

Mr. Toby Price

Parent, educator, and author of
The Almost True Adventures of Tytus the Monkey
(Yes, he's that assistant principal fired for reading *I Need a New Butt!*)

Knock, Knock, New Friend

Welcome to the hooting-and-hollering, LOL land of knock-knocks and silly stories, where you're sure to laugh your socks off!

One cool thing about jokes and silly stories is the way they play with words. As you read, see if you can spot the wordplay. When you use words in creative ways, you'll find yourself bending sounds to make new meaning and exploring funny ways to think about how we understand things. See, jokes are funny, but being funny also means being clever!

In case you like treasure hunts, here's a map of the book: In the beginning, there's a boatload of knock-knock jokes. Later, you'll find hilarious stories that get longer as you go. You can start by reading the shorter jokes, then work your way up to those with a big, long, belly-bubbling punch line!

But here's the thing: this book is also sort of like a choose-your-own-adventure. You can start at the beginning, middle, or end. You'll giggle (and maybe even snort!) your way to gold no matter what road you take! So gather 'round, or snuggle up, and get prepared to tickle lots of funny bones along the way.

No one knows for sure where knock-knock jokes first came from. Some people think that Shakespeare wrote the first knock-knock joke in one of his plays—over 400 years ago! Others say it came from a kids' game. Either way, the knock-knock joke is definitely here to stay. Let's get to knockin'.

Knock, knock.

Who's there?

Oswald.

Oswald who?

Oswald my bubble gum!

Knock, knock.

Who's there?

Sadie.

Sadie who?

Sadie magic word and watch me disappear.

Knock, knock.

Who's there?

Amos.

Amos who?

Amos-quito!

Knock, knock.

Who's there?

Anudder.

Anudder who?

Anudder mosquito!

Knock, knock.

Who's there?

Noah.

Noah who?

Noah good place we can play tag?

Knock, knock.

Who's there?

Joanna.

Joanna who?

Joanna build a fort?

Knock, knock.

Who's there?

Ash.

Ash who?

Sounds like you have a cold!

Knock, knock.

Who's there?

Nadia.

Nadia who?

Nadia head if you understand me.

Knock, knock.

Who's there?

Jess.

Jess who?

Jess cut the talking and come hang!

Knock, knock.
Who's there?
Rufus.
Rufus who?
**Rufus the most important
part of your house.**

Knock, knock.
Who's there?
Otto.
Otto who?
Otto know. I forgot.

Knock, knock.
Who's there?
Arfur.
Arfur who?
Arfur got again!

Knock, knock.

Who's there?

Carmen.

Carmen who?

Carmen get it!

Knock, knock.

Who's there?

Reed.

Reed who?

Redo? OK . . . Knock, knock.

Knock, knock.

Who's there?

Alice.

Alice who?

Alice so quiet. Let's make some noise!

Knock, knock.

Who's there?

Susan.

Susan who?

Susan socks go on your feet!

Knock, knock.

Who's there?

Tyrone.

Tyrone who?

Tyrone shoelaces!

Knock, knock.

Who's there?

Ben.

Ben who?

Ben looking for some tasty spaghetti.

Knock, knock.

Who's there?

Ada.

Ada who?

Ada great sandwich for lunch today.

Knock, knock.

Who's there?

Erin.

Erin who?

Let some Erin here, it's hot!

Knock, knock.

Who's there?

Cher.

Cher who?

Cher would be nice if you opened the door!

Knock, knock.

Who's there?

Keanu.

Keanu who?

Keanu let me in, there's a rainstorm!

Knock, knock.

Who's there?

Alec.

Alec who?

Alec it when you ask me questions.

Knock, knock.

Who's there?

Czar.

Czar who?

Czar a doctor in the house?

Knock, knock.

Who's there?

Brett.

Brett who?

Brett you don't know who this is.

Knock, knock.

Who's there?

Norma Lee.

Norma Lee who?

**Norma Lee I ring the doorbell,
but yours is broken!**

Knock, knock.

Who's there?

Abby.

Abby who?

Abby birthday to you!

Knock, knock.

Who's there?

Sue.

Sue who?

Sue-prise! Here's a birthday cake.

Knock, knock.

Who's there?

Howard.

Howard who?

Howard I know?

Knock, knock.

Who's there?

Andrew.

Andrew who?

Andrew a picture!

Knock, knock.

Who's there?

Dejav.

Dejav who?

Knock, knock.

Knock, knock.

Who's there?

Michelle.

Michelle who?

Michelle has a hermit crab inside!

Knock, knock.

Who's there?

Anita.

Anita who?

Anita go to the bathroom!

Knock, knock.
Who's there?
Billy Bob Joe Penny.
Billy Bob Joe Penny who?
Really? How many Billy Bob Joe Pennys do you know?

Knock, knock.
Who's there?
Mike Snifferpippet.
Mike Snifferpippet who?
Oh, come on, how many Mike Snifferpippets do you know?

Knock, knock.
Who's there?
Althea.
Althea who?
Althea later, alligator!

Knock, knock.

Who's there?

Ida.

Ida who?

I think it's pronounced "Idaho."

Knock, knock.

Who's there?

Dwayne.

Dwayne who?

Dwayne the bathtub, it's time for bed!

Knock, knock.

Who's there?

Annie.

Annie who?

Annie body home?

Knock, knock.

Who's there?

Iva.

Iva who?

Iva sore hand from knocking!

Knock, knock.

Who's there?

Candice.

Candice who?

Candice joke get any worse?!

Knock, knock.

Who's there?

Brad.

Brad who?

Brad news, I'm afraid.

Knock, knock.

Who's there?

Juno.

Juno who?

Juno that I'm out here, right?

Knock, knock.

Who's there?

Ray D.

Ray D. who?

Ray D. or not, here I come.

Knock, knock.

Who's there?

Iris.

Iris who?

Iris you would let me in.

Knock, knock.

Who's there?

Al.

Al who?

Al be home for the holidays.

Knock, knock.

Who's there?

Sherwood.

Sherwood who?

Sherwood like to go to the movies!

Knock, knock.

Who's there?

Hannah.

Hannah who?

Hannah partridge in a pear tree.

Knock, knock.

Who's there?

Vera.

Vera who?

Vera few people like stinky cheese!

Knock, knock.

Who's there?

Ahmed.

Ahmed who?

Ahmed a mistake, give me an eraser.

Knock, knock.

Who's there?

Leon.

Leon who?

Leon me when you're not strong!

Knock, knock.

Who's there?

Sarah.

Sarah who?

Sarah phone I could use?

Knock, knock.

Who's there?

Justin.

Justin who?

Justin time for dinner!

Knock, knock.

Who's there?

Theodore.

Theodore who?

Theodore wasn't open so I had to knock.

Knock, knock.

Who's there?

Luke.

Luke who?

Luke who got a Valentine!

Knock, knock.

Who's there?

Keith.

Keith who?

Keith me, my thweet prince!

Knock, knock.

Who's there?

Phil.

Phil who?

Phil up the tire. It needs more air.

Knock, knock.

Who's there?

Iona.

Iona who?

Iona new bike!

Knock, knock.

Who's there?

Carl.

Carl who?

Carl get you there faster than a bike, silly.

Knock, knock.

Who's there?

Bruce.

Bruce who?

Bruce easily, gotta wear kneepads!

Knock, knock.

Who's there?

Kent.

Kent who?

Kent you tell by my voice?

Knock, knock.

Who's there?

Watson.

Watson who?

Watson TV right now?

Knock, knock.

Who's there?

Nicholas.

Nicholas who?

A Nicholas not much money these days.

Knock, knock.

Who's there?

Stu.

Stu who?

Stu late to come out and play?

Knock, knock.

Who's there?

Ivor.

Ivor who?

Ivor you let me in, or I'll go play next door.

Knock, knock.

Who's there?

Teddy.

Teddy who?

Teddy is the first day of school!

Knock, knock.

Who's there?

Abie.

Abie who?

Abie C D E F G . . .

Knock, knock.

Who's there?

Rita.

Rita who?

Rita book, you might learn something!

Knock, knock.

Who's there?

Shelby.

Shelby who?

Shelby comin' 'round the mountain when she comes!

Knock, knock.

Who's there?

Will.

Will who?

Will you open the door?

Knock, knock.

Who's there?

Mikey.

Mikey who?

Mikey doesn't fit in the keyhole!

Knock, knock.

Who's there?

Frank.

Frank who?

Frank you for coming to the door!

Knock, knock.

Who's there?

Ferdie.

Ferdie who?

Ferdie last time, open this door!

Knock, knock.

Who's there?

Alex.

Alex who?

Alex plain later.

Knock, knock.

Who's there?

Hope.

Hope who?

Hope you can still laugh at a good joke.

Knock, knock.

Who's there?

Lena.

Lena who?

Lena a little closer, and I'll tell you another joke!

Knock, knock.

Who's there?

Haven.

Haven who?

Haven you heard enough of these knock-knock jokes?

Knock, knock.

Who's there?

Saul.

Saul who?

Saul there is—there ain't no more!

Knock, knock.

Who's there?

Bacon.

Bacon who?

Bacon some cookies in there?
It smells delicious!

Knock, knock.

Who's there?

Figs.

Figs who?

Figs the doorbell!

Knock, knock.

Who's there?

Icing.

Icing who?

Icing so loudly my neighbors can hear me.

Knock, knock.

Who's there?

Butter.

Butter who?

Butter be quick, I have to get home.

Knock, knock.

Who's there?

Honeydew.

Honeydew who?

Honeydew you wanna pickle?

Knock, knock.

Who's there?

Quiche.

Quiche who?

Quiche your granny good night.

Knock, knock.

Who's there?

Falafel.

Falafel who?

Falafel my skateboard and landed on my knee.

Knock, knock.

Who's there?

Doughnut.

Doughnut who?

Doughnut ask, and I won't tell!

Knock, knock.

Who's there?

Curry.

Curry who?

Curry me back home, will you?!

Knock, knock.

Who's there?

Turnip.

Turnip who?

Turnip the volume, I love this song!

Knock, knock.

Who's there?

Gouda.

Gouda who?

Gouda knock-knock jokes, don't you think?

Knock, knock.

Who's there?

Beef.

Beef who?

Beef-ore I get cold, you'd better let me in.

Knock, knock.

Who's there?

Carrot.

Carrot who?

Carrot-e CHOP!

Knock, knock.

Who's there?

Banana.

Banana who?

Knock, knock.

Who's there?

Banana.

Banana who?

Knock, knock.

Who's there?

Orange.

Orange who?

Orange you glad I didn't say banana?

Knock, knock.

Who's there?

Ketchup.

Ketchup who?

Ketchup with me, and I'll tell you!

Knock, knock.

Who's there?

Cheese.

Cheese who?

For cheese a jolly good fellow!

Knock, knock.

Who's there?

Pecan.

Pecan who?

Pecan someone your own size.

Knock, knock.

Who's there?

Kiwi.

Kiwi who?

Kiwi go to the store?

Knock, knock.

Who's there?

Lettuce.

Lettuce who?

Lettuce in, it's cold outside!

Knock, knock.

Who's there?

Two knee.

Two knee who?

Two knee fish sandwich, please.

Knock, knock.

Who's there?

Pudding.

Pudding who?

Pudding on your shoes before your pants is a bad idea.

Knock, knock.

Who's there?

Eggs.

Eggs who?

Well, eggs-cuuuuse me.

Knock, knock.

Who's there?

Zany.

Zany who?

Zany body want a cupcake?

Knock, knock.

Who's there?

Peas.

Peas who?

Peas to meet you!

Knock, knock.

Who's there?

Cantaloupe.

Cantaloupe who?

Cantaloupe to Vegas until we're grown-ups!

Knock, knock.

Who's there?

Olive.

Olive who?

Olive next door. Hi, neighbor!

Knock, knock.

Who's there?

Pasta.

Pasta who?

Pasta salt and pepper, please.

Knock, knock.

Who's there?

Taco.

Taco who?

Taco you later.

Knock, knock.

Who's there?

Ice cream.

Ice cream who?

ICE CREAM SO YOU CAN HEAR ME!

Knock, knock.

Who's there?

Omelet.

Omelet who?

Omelet you finish.

Knock, knock.

Who's there?

Soda.

Soda who?

Soda answer is still no?

Knock, knock.

Who's there?

Mushroom.

Mushroom who?

There's mushroom for improvement on this doorbell!

Knock, knock.

Who's there?

Cook.

Cook who?

Yeah, that does sound a little cuckoo!

Knock, knock.

Who's there?

Pizza.

Pizza who?

Pizza nice guy once you get to know him.

Knock, knock.

Who's there?

Goat.

Goat who?

Goat to the door and find out.

Knock, knock.

Who's there?

Alpaca.

Alpaca who?

Alpaca the trunk, you pack the suitcase.

Knock, knock.

Who's there?

Pooch.

Pooch who?

Pooch your arms up in the air, wave them like you just don't care.

Knock, knock.

Who's there?

Beezer.

Beezer who?

Beezer good at making honey.

Knock, knock.

Who's there?

Giraffe.

Giraffe who?

Giraffe anything to eat? I'm starving!

Knock, knock.

Who's there?

Cow.

Cow who?

No, cow says mooooo!

Knock, knock.

Who's there?

Moose.

Moose who?

Moose you be so nosy?

Knock, knock.

Who's there?

Aardvark.

Aardvark who?

Aardvark a hundred miles for you.

Knock, knock.

Who's there?

Gorilla.

Gorilla who?

Gorilla burger, I've got the buns and the relish!

Knock, knock.

Who's there?

Halibut.

Halibut who?

Halibut lending me five dollars?

Knock, knock.

Who's there?

Chicken.

Chicken who?

Chicken your pockets. I think the keys are in there.

Knock, knock.

Who's there?

Honeybee.

Honeybee who?

Honeybee a dear and open the door, will you?

Knock, knock.

Who's there?

Iguana.

Iguana who?

Iguana hold your hand.

Knock, knock.

Who's there?

Interrupting cow.

Interruptin—

Mooooo!

Knock, knock.

Who's there?

Interrupting sloth.

Interrupting sloth who?

(20 seconds of silence) Slooooooooooth.

Knock, knock.

Who's there?

Bumblebee.

Bumblebee who?

Bumblebee cold if you don't wear pants!

Knock, knock.

Who's there?

Lion.

Lion who?

Lion on the floor waiting for you to open the door!

Knock, knock.

Who's there?

T. rex.

T. rex who?

There is a T. rex at your door, and you want to know its name?!

Knock, knock.

Who's there?

Yukon.

Yukon who?

Yukon say that again!

Knock, knock.

Who's there?

Ruff, ruff.

Ruff, ruff who?

Who let the dogs out? I heard barking!

Knock, knock.

Who's there?

Mammoth.

Mammoth who?

Mammoth is sthuck 'cause I'th been eatin' peanut buther.

Knock, knock.

Who's there?

A herd.

A herd who?

A herd you were home, so here I am!

Knock, knock.

Who's there?

Toucan.

Toucan who?

Toucan play this game!

Knock, knock.

Who's there?

Cattle.

Cattle who?

Cattle purr if you pet her.

Knock, knock.

Who's there?

Owls say.

Owls say who?

Yes, they do.

Knock, knock.

Who's there?

Toad.

Toad who?

Toad you I knew a good knock-knock joke!

Knock, knock.

Who's there?

Horsp.

Horsp who?

Did you just say "horse poo"?

Knock, knock.

Who's there?

Whale.

Whale who?

Whale, I guess I'm at the wrong house.

Knock, knock.

Who's there?

Schnauzer.

Schnauzer who?

Schnauzer day going?

Knock, knock.

Who's there?

Kanga.

Kanga who?

No, it's kanga*roo*!

Knock, knock.

Who's there?

Roach.

Roach who?

Roach you a note last week. Gonna answer?

Knock, knock.

Who's there?

Meow.

Meow who?

Take meow to the ball game.

Knock, knock.

Who's there?

Ooze.

Ooze who?

Ooze a good dog?

Knock, knock.

Who's there?

Viper.

Viper who?

Viper nose, it's running!

Knock, knock.

Who's there?

Some bunny.

Some bunny who?

Some bunny has been eating all my veggies.

Knock, knock.

Who's there?

Rhino.

Rhino who?

Rhino every knock-knock joke there is!

Knock, knock.

Who's there?

Beaver.

Beaver who?

Beaver-y quiet, the teacher is coming!

Knock, knock.

Who's there?

Who.

Who who?

Is there an owl in here?!

Knock, knock.

Who's there?

Hatch.

Hatch who?

Bless you.

Knock, knock.

Who's there?

Oink, oink.

Oink, oink who?

Make up your mind—are you a pig or an owl?

Knock, knock.

Who's there?

Howl.

Howl who?

Howl you know it's really me unless you open the door?

Knock, knock.

Who's there?

Daisy.

Daisy who?

Daisy me rollin', they hatin'.

Knock, knock.

Who's there?

A little old lady.

A little old lady who?

Wow, I didn't know you could yodel!

Knock, knock.

Who's there?

Granny.

Granny who?

Knock, knock.

Who's there?

Granny.

Granny who?

Knock, knock.

Who's there?

Aunt.

Aunt who?

Aunt you glad Granny's gone home?

Knock, knock.

Who's there?

Nana.

Nana who?

Nana your business!

Knock, knock.

Who's there?

FBI.

FBI who?

We're asking the questions here.

Knock, knock.

Who's there?

Police.

Police who?

Police let us in, we want a snack!

Knock, knock.

Who's there?

Burglar.

Burglar who?

Burglars don't knock!

Knock, knock.

Who's there?

Watts.

Watts who?

Watts up, doc?

Knock, knock.

Who's there?

Warrior.

Warrior who?

Warrior been all my life?

Knock, knock.

Who's there?

Army.

Army who?

Army and you still hungry?

Knock, knock.

Who's there?

Cargo.

Cargo who?

Cargo "Beep, beep! Vroom, vroom!"

Knock, knock.

Who's there?

Tank.

Tank who?

You're welcome!

Knock, knock.

Who's there?

Pikachu.

Pikachu who?

Pikachu presents and you'll be in trouble.

Knock, knock.

Who's there?

Scooby.

Scooby who?

Scooby Doo, of course!

Knock, knock.

Who's there?

Tinker Bell.

Tinker Bell who?

Tinker Bell isn't working so I had to knock.

Knock, knock.

Who's there?

Barbie.

Barbie who?

Barbie-cue sauce! Got any extra?

Knock, knock.

Who's there?

Toyota.

Toyota who?

Toyota be a law against these jokes!

Knock, knock.

Who's there?

King Tut.

King Tut who?

King Tut-key Fried Chicken!

Knock, knock.

Who's there?

Sherlock.

Sherlock who?

Sherlock your door tight.

Knock, knock.

Who's there?

Goliath.

Goliath who?

Goliath down, you looketh tired!

Knock, knock.

Who's there?

Champ.

Champ who?

Champ-oo cleans dirty hair!

Knock, knock.

Who's there?

Gargoyle.

Gargoyle who?

Gargoyle with salt water and your throat will feel better!

Knock, knock.

Who's there?

A little kid.

A little kid who?

A little kid who can't reach the doorbell.

Knock, knock.

Who's there?

Interrupting doctor.

Interrupting doc—

You have a broken leg!

Knock, knock.
Who's there?
Interrupting pirate.
Interrupting pi—
ARRRRRRRR!

Knock, knock.
Who's there?
Witches.
Witches who?
**Witches the way
to the store?**

Knock, knock.
Who's there?
Elf.
Elf who?
Elf me wrap this present!

Knock, knock.

Who's there?

Vampire.

Vampire who?

Vampire State Building!

Knock, knock.

Who's there?

Fangs.

Fangs who?

Fangs for letting me in.

Knock, knock.

Who's there?

Wand.

Wand who?

Wand to come out and play?

Knock, knock.

Who's there?

Voodoo.

Voodoo who?

Voodoo you think you are asking me so many questions?

Knock, knock.

Who's there?

Armageddon.

Armageddon who?

Armageddon a little bored. Let's go play!

Knock, knock.

Who's there?

An extraterrestrial.

An extraterrestrial who?

Wait, how many extraterrestrials do you know?

Knock, knock.

Who's there?

Jupiter.

Jupiter who?

Jupiter fly in my soup?

Knock, knock.

Who's there?

Disk.

Disk who?

Disk is a recording, please leave your message after the beep!

Knock, knock.

Who's there?

Icon.

Icon who?

Icon tell more knock-knock jokes than you can.

Knock, knock.

Who's there?

Comb.

Comb who?

Comb on down, and I'll tell you!

Knock, knock.

Who's there?

Razor.

Razor who?

Razor hand up if you like dogs!

Knock, knock.

Who's there?

Needle.

Needle who?

Needle little help getting in the door!

Knock, knock.

Who's there?

A broken pencil.

A broken pencil who?

Never mind, it's pointless.

Knock, knock.

Who's there?

Wooden shoe.

Wooden shoe who?

Wooden shoe like to know!

Knock, knock.

Who's there?

Cotton.

Cotton who?

Cotton mud. Please help me!

Knock, knock.

Who's there?

Wire.

Wire who?

Wire you always asking who's there?

Knock, knock.

Who's there?

Leash.

Leash who?

Leash you could do is open the door.

Knock, knock.

Who's there?

Defense.

Defense who?

Defense has a hole in it, so our dog got loose.

Knock, knock.

Who's there?

CD.

CD who?

CD dog around the corner?

Knock, knock.

Who's there?

Radio.

Radio who?

Radio not, here I come!

Knock, knock.

Who's there?

Stopwatch.

Stopwatch who?

Stopwatch you're doing and let me in!

Knock, knock.

Who's there?

Guitar.

Guitar who?

Guitar coats, it's cold outside!

Knock, knock.

Who's there?

Thermos.

Thermos who?

Thermos be a better way to talk to you.

Knock, knock.

Who's there?

Cash.

Cash who?

No thanks, but I'll take a peanut if you have one!

Knock, knock.

Who's there?

Money.

Money who?

Money hurts when I run.

Knock, knock.

Who's there?

Triton.

Triton who?

Triton tell you a joke here!

Knock, knock.

Who's there?

Bed.

Bed who?

Bed you can't guess who it is!

Knock, knock.

Who's there?

Chimney.

Chimney who?

Chimney cricket! Have you seen Pinocchio?

Knock, knock.

Who's there?

Dishes.

Dishes who?

Dishes a nice place you got here.

Knock, knock.

Who's there?

Window.

Window who?

Window we eat?

Knock, knock.

Who's there?

Avenue.

Avenue who?

Avenue heard this joke before?

Knock, knock.

Who's there?

Pasture.

Pasture who?

Pasture bedtime, isn't it?

Knock, knock.

Who's there?

Hike.

Hike who?

I didn't know you liked Japanese poetry!

Knock, knock.

Who's there?

Tennis.

Tennis who?

Tennis five plus five!

Knock, knock.

Who's there?

Canoe.

Canoe who?

Canoe come out and play?

Knock, knock.

Who's there?

Yacht.

Yacht who?

Yacht to know me by now!

Knock, knock.

Who's there?

Acid.

Acid who?

Acid sit down—you're rocking the boat.

Knock, knock.

Who's there?

Kelp.

Kelp who?

Kelp me. I can't swim!

Knock, knock.
Who's there?
Wheelbarrow.
Wheelbarrow who?
Wheelbarrow your scooter and basketball, please!

Knock, knock.
Who's there?
Cactus.
Cactus who?
Cactus makes perfect.

Knock, knock.
Who's there?
A leaf.
A leaf who?
A leaf you alone if you leaf me alone.

Knock, knock.

Who's there?

Shore.

Shore who?

Shore hope you love these knock-knock jokes!

Knock, knock.

Who's there?

Water.

Water who?

Water you asking so many questions for, just open up!

Knock, knock.

Who's there?

Snow.

Snow who?

Snow use. I forgot my name again!

Knock, knock.

Who's there?

Accordion.

Accordion who?

Accordion to the weather person, it's going to rain tomorrow!

Knock, knock.

Who's there?

Icy.

Icy who?

Icy you looking at me!

Knock, knock.

Who's there?

Frostbite.

Frostbite who?

Frostbite your food, then chew it!

Knock, knock.

Who's there?

Senior.

Senior who?

Senior so nosy, I'm not going to tell you.

Knock, knock.

Who's there?

Major.

Major who?

Major day with this joke, I bet!

Knock, knock.

Who's there?

Art.

Art who?

R2-D2.

Knock, knock.

Who's there?

Spell.

Spell who?

W-H-O.

Knock, knock.

Who's there?

To.

To who?

No, it's "to *whom*"!

Knock, knock.

Who's there?

Double.

Double who?

W!

Knock, knock.

Who's there?

One.

One who?

One, two, three. Testing. One, two, three.

Knock, knock.

Who's there?

Dozen.

Dozen who?

Dozen anyone want to let me in?

Knock, knock.

Who's there?

Ratio.

Ratio who?

Ratio to the end of the street!

Knock, knock.

Who's there?

Ears.

Ears who?

Ears another knock-knock joke for you!

Knock, knock.

Who's there?

Mustache.

Mustache who?

**Mustache you a question, but
I'll shave it for later!**

Knock, knock.

Who's there?

Zoom.

Zoom who?

Zoom did you expect?

Knock, knock.

Who's there?

Eyesore.

Eyesore who?

Eyesore do like you!

Knock, knock.

Who's there?

Noise.

Noise who?

Noise to see you!

Knock, knock.

Who's there?

Echo.

Echo who?

WHO. WHO. WHO. WHO.

WHO. WHO. WHO.

Knock, knock.

Who's there?

Europe.

Europe who?

No, you're a poo!

Knock, knock.

Who's there?

A Mayan.

A Mayan who?

A Mayan the way?

Knock, knock.

Who's there?

Havana.

Havana who?

**Havana wonderful time.
Wish you were here!**

Knock, knock.

Who's there?

Amarillo.

Amarillo who?

Amarillo nice kid.

Knock, knock.

Who's there?

Juneau.

Juneau who?

Juneau the capital of Alaska?

Knock, knock.

Who's there?

Hawaii.

Hawaii who?

I'm fine, Hawaii you?

Knock, knock.

Who's there?

Utah.

Utah who?

Utah-king to me?

Knock, knock.

Who's there?

Kenya.

Kenya who?

Kenya feel the love tonight?

Knock, knock.

Who's there?

Oslo.

Oslo who?

Oslo down, what's the hurry?!

Knock, knock.

Who's there?

India.

India who?

India nighttime I go to sleep.

Knock, knock.

Who's there?

Sweden.

Sweden who?

Sweden sour chicken!

Knock, knock.
Who's there?
June.
June who?
June know how long I've been knocking out here?

Knock, knock.
Who's there?
August.
August who?
August of wind blew my hat off.

Knock, knock.

Who's there?

Venice.

Venice who?

Venice your mom coming home?

Knock, knock.

Who's there?

Weekend.

Weekend who?

Weekend do anything we want!

Knock, knock.

Who's there?

Scold.

Scold who?

Scold outside, let me in!

Knock, knock.

Who's there?

Thumping.

Thumping who?

Thumping green and slimy is climbing up your back!

Knock, knock.

Who's there?

Closure.

Closure who?

Closure mouth while you're chewing!

Knock, knock.

Who's there?

Foster.

Foster who?

Foster than the speed of light!

Knock, knock.

Who's there?

Adore.

Adore who?

Adore is between you and me, so please open up!

Knock, knock.

Who's there?

Passion.

Passion who?

Passion through and thought I'd say hello.

Knock, knock.

Who's there?

Knock, knock.

Who's there?

Knock, knock.

Who's there?

Doorbell repair person.

Knock, knock.

Who's there?

Handsome.

Handsome who?

Handsome crackers through the keyhole and I'll tell you.

Knock, knock.

Who's there?

Nobel.

Nobel who?

There's Nobel, that's why I knocked!

Knock, knock.

Who's there?

I love.

I love who?

I love you too!

Knock, knock.
Who's there?
Bless.
Bless who?
I didn't sneeze!

Knock, knock.
Who's there?
Howdy.
Howdy who?
Howdy-licious are those cookies?

Knock, knock.
Who's there?
Nobody.
Nobody who?
. . . (silence).

Knock, knock.

Who's there?

You.

You who?

You-hoo, anybody home?

Will you remember me in a year?

Yes.

Will you remember me in a month?

Yes.

Will you remember me in a week?

Yes.

Knock, knock.

Who's there?

You already forgot me?!

Knock, knock.

Who's there?

I am.

I am who?

Don't you even know who you are?!

Knock, knock.

Who's there?

Bam.

Bam who?

Bam who is what pandas eat.
Let's go out for pizza.

Knock, knock.

Who's there?

I. O.

I. O. who?

Me! When are you paying me back?

Knock, knock.

Who's there?

Peeka.

Peeka who?

Oh, there you are!

Knock, knock.

Who's there?

Chooch.

Chooch who?

All aboard!

Knock, knock.

Who's there?

I need a puh.

I need a puh who?

Then you should find a bathroom!

Knock, knock.

Who's there?

Boo.

Boo who?

Please don't cry. It's only a joke.

Knock, knock.

Who's there?

Tiss.

Tiss who?

A tiss-who is for blowing your nose.

Knock, knock.

Who's there?

Weirdo.

Weirdo who?

Weirdo you think you're going?

Knock, knock.

Who's there?

Woo.

Woo who?

Glad you're excited for the party!

Knock, knock.

Who's there?

Juicy.

Juicy who?

Juicy what I saw?

Knock, knock.

Who's there?

Yeah.

Yeah who?

Wow, I'm happy to see you too!

Knock, knock.

Who's there?

Shamp.

Shamp who?

Does my hair really look that dirty?

Knock, knock.

Who's there?

Poop.

Poop who?

Ha ha, you just said poo-poo!

Knock, knock.

Who's there?

Ho, ho.

Ho, ho who?

Your Santa impression could use a little work.

Knock, knock.

Who's there?

Nuisance.

Nuisance who?

What's nuisance yesterday?

Knock, knock.

Who's there?

Smell mop.

Smell mop who?

Ew, no thanks!

Knock, knock.

Who's there?

Pee.

Pee who?

Pee-yew!

SILLY STORIES

Next up are some sidesplitting silly stories, a.k.a. jokes with a longer setup. Most of the stories play on funny relationships and misunderstandings between people. Others rely on goofy wordplay to make you giggle. You'll find jokes that get to the punch line quick, and jokes that take you on a journey to a hilarious conclusion that is worth the wait. Did you hear about that time you told a bunch of jokes? Time to get crackin'!

Whoever invented knock-knock jokes should get a no-bell prize.

· ·

I couldn't figure out why the baseball kept getting larger. Then it hit me.

· ·

I don't trust those trees. They seem kind of shady.

· ·

Have you heard the story of the magic sandwich? Never mind, it's just a bunch of bologna.

· ·

Want to hear a joke about paper? Never mind, it's tearable.

If your refrigerator is running,
you should try to catch it!

. . . .

Simba was moving too slowly,
so I told him to Mufasa!

. . . .

Wanna hear a joke about construction?
Never mind, I'm still working on it.

. . . .

My parents are giving away our chimney
for free. You could say it's on the house.

. . . .

I swallowed a dictionary. It gave
me thesaurus throat I ever had.

We have a field trip to the soda factory today. I hope there isn't a pop quiz.

....

Have you ever tried to eat a clock? It's very time-consuming.

....

Two fish are in a tank. One turns to the other and says, "How do you drive this thing?"

....

PATIENT: Doctor, my nose is 11 inches long!
DOCTOR: Come back when it grows into a foot!

Spring is here. I'm so excited
I wet my plants!

....

There are two muffins in an oven.
One muffin turns to the other muffin
and says, "Gee, it's hot in here."
The other muffin says, "OH MY
GOSH! A TALKING MUFFIN!"

After many years, a prisoner is finally released. He runs around yelling, "I'm free! I'm free!" A little kid walks up to him and says, "So what? I'm four."

. . . .

Two friends meet on opposite sides of a river. One shouts to the other, "I need you to help me get to the other side." The other friend replies, "You're *on* the other side!"

. . . .

JANELLE: I just fell off a fifty-foot ladder.
ELISA: Oh my goodness, are you OK?
JANELLE: Yeah, I fell off the first step.

Shay walks into a pet store and asks for a dozen bees. The clerk carefully counts out 13 bees onto the counter. "That's one too many!" says Shay. The clerk replies, "It's a freebie."

....

I got fired from my job at the bank today. Someone came in and asked me to check their balance, so I pushed them over.

....

Have you heard the one about the student who was afraid of negative numbers? He'll stop at nothing to avoid them.

Once upon a time there was a king who was only 12 inches tall. He was a terrible king, but he made a great ruler.

....

NURSE: The invisible man is here for his appointment.
DOCTOR: Tell him I'm sorry I can't see him right now.

....

Did you hear about the guy whose whole left side was cut off? He's all right now.

....

Two artists had a contest.
It ended in a draw.

I told my friend I was going to make a bike out of spaghetti. She couldn't believe it when I rode pasta.

. . . .

A mom and her son come home from the grocery store. The boy immediately empties out a box of animal crackers and the mom asks him why. The boy says, "It says 'do not eat if seal is broken,' so I'm looking for the seal."

. . . .

LANA: Dad, there's a hole in my shoe.
DAD: Yes, Lana, that's where you put your foot.

A kid finds a magic lamp. He rubs the lamp, and a genie appears and says, "What is your first wish?" The kid says, "I wish I were rich!" The genie replies, "It's done! What's your second wish, Rich?"

....

TEACHER: What is the chemical formula for water?
STUDENT: HIJKLMNO.
TEACHER: What are you talking about?
STUDENT: Yesterday you said it's H to O!

....

I woke up this morning and ran around the block five times. Then I got tired, so I picked up the block and put it back in the toy box.

Two windmills are standing in a wind farm. One asks, "What's your favorite type of music?" The other says, "I'm a big metal fan."

....

BIANCA: Why do elephants wear red nail polish?
MALIA: I don't know, why?
BIANCA: To hide in cherry trees.
MALIA: But I've never seen an elephant in a cherry tree.
BIANCA: See, it works!

....

A parent called his child's doctor. "Hello! My child just swallowed my pen. What should I do?" The doctor replied, "Write with another pen!"

A woman walks into a library, approaches the librarian, and says, "I'll have a cheeseburger and fries, please." The librarian says, "Ma'am, you know you're in a library, right?" "Sorry," she whispers. "I'll have a cheeseburger and fries, please."

For a while, Houdini used a trapdoor in every single show he did. I guess you could say he was going through a stage.

....

DAD: Can I see your report card, son?
MANISH: I don't have it.
DAD: Why not?
MANISH: I gave it to my friend. He wanted to scare his parents.

....

One day Mateo went to see Caleb. Caleb had a big swollen nose. "Whoa, what happened, Caleb?" Mateo asked. "I sniffed a brose," Caleb replied. "What?" Mateo said. "There's no *b* in 'rose'!" Caleb replied, "There was in this one!"

Alonzo asks his father, "Dad, are bugs
good to eat?" "That's gross! Don't talk
about things like that over dinner,"
Alonzo's dad replies. After dinner his father
asks, "Now, son, what were you asking
me?" "Oh, nothing," Alonzo says. "There
was a bug in your soup, but you ate it."

A waiter gives a man a cup of coffee. The man takes a sip and spits it out. He turns to the waiter and says, "Waiter! This coffee tastes like mud!" The waiter, looking surprised, turns to the man and says, "But, sir, it's fresh ground!"

. . . .

Emerson and Finley are hiking through the woods when Emerson cries out, "Snake! Run!" Finley laughs and says, "Oh, relax. It's only a baby. Can't you hear its rattle?"

. . . .

A polar bear walks into a restaurant and says, "I'll have a sandwich and . . . chips." The waiter asks, "Why the big pause?" The polar bear replies, "I don't know, I've always had them."

A man was walking down the street and saw a sign in a store window that said "Help Wanted," so the man ran into the store and yelled out, "What's wrong?!"

....

Adalynn and Olivia are on a cruise. Adalynn says, "It's awfully quiet on deck tonight." Olivia replies, "That's because everyone is watching the band tonight." Surprised, Adalynn corrects her, "There isn't a band playing tonight." Olivia responds, "That's funny. I could've sworn I heard someone say 'a band on ship.'"

A mom texts her child, "Hi! Willow, what does IDK, LY & TTYL mean?" Willow texts back, "I Don't Know, Love You & Talk to You Later." The mom texts, "It's OK, don't worry about it. I'll ask your sister, love you too."

. . . .

Halle arrives late to school. Her teacher asks her why she's late. She says, "Because of the sign." The teacher asks, "What sign?" Halle replies, "The one that says, 'School ahead, go slow.'"

. . . .

Marcella went to a 24-hour grocery store. When she got there, the owner was locking the front door. Marcella said, "Hey! The sign says you're open twenty-four hours." The owner said, "Yes, but not in a row!"

"Luciano, why do deep-sea divers always sit on the side of the boat with air tanks on their backs, and fall backward out of the boat?" Luciano thinks for a minute, then says, "That's easy. Because if they fell forward, they'd still be in the boat!"

. . . .

A teacher asked her students to use the word *beans* in a sentence. "My mother grows beans," said one girl. "My father cooks beans," said a boy. A third student spoke up, "We are all human beans."

. . . .

"Mommy, Hassan just broke the bedroom window!" "Oh no! How did that happen?" "I threw a ball to him, and he ducked."

COACH: Why are you late for the game?
CATERPILLAR: I had to put my shoes on.

....

Alonzo and his dad went back to the same restaurant. This time, Alonzo's dad flagged down the waiter and said, "Excuse me, but I have a bee in my soup." The waiter replied, "Yes, sir. Didn't you order the alphabet soup this time?"

....

TEACHER: If you had one dollar and you asked your dad for another, how many dollars would you have?
DANTE: One dollar.
TEACHER: You don't know your math.
DANTE: You don't know my dad.

A helicopter pilot was lost. He saw a group of hikers below and held up a sign that read, "Where am I?" The hikers answered with their own sign. It read, "You're in a helicopter."

It was a baby mosquito's first day flying alone. When the mosquito came home later that day, his father asked, "How was your journey?" The baby mosquito replied, "It went great. Everyone was clapping for me!"

Two brothers were sitting in a kayak. They were chilly, so they lit a fire. Unsurprisingly, the boat sank, proving once again that you can't have your kayak and heat it too.

PATIENT: Doctor, I keep dreaming I'm in a washing machine.

DOCTOR: What happens?

PATIENT: I toss and turn all night.

....

One day Siobhan came home early from school and her mom asked, "Why are you home so early?" She answered, "Because I was the only one who answered a question correctly in my class." Her mom said, "Wow, my daughter is a genius! What was the question?" Siobhan replied, "Did you squirt ketchup packets all over the cafeteria floor?"

....

ESME: My parents just got a new computer for my sister.

RYAN: I wish my parents could make that kind of a trade for my sister.

There were three monsters in the desert. They all brought something to cool them down. Mariana brought a parasol. Floyd brought a canteen. Paul brought a car door. Mariana asked Paul, "Why do you have a car door?" Paul said, "So we can roll the window down when we get hot!"

How many kids does it take to clean a bedroom? Three. One to say, "But all I do is sleep in there!" and two to say, "But we did it last time!"

....

Odin complained, "I have a stomachache!" "It's because your stomach's empty," Odin's mother replied. "You'd feel better if you had something in it." That afternoon, Odin's dad complained that he had a headache all day. Odin perked up. "It's because it's empty," he said. "You'd feel better if you had something in it!"

JACK: What's the difference between a tuna, a piano, and a glue stick?

FERNANDO: I don't know. What?

JACK: You can tuna piano, but you can't piano a tuna.

FERNANDO: What about the glue stick?

JACK: I knew you'd get stuck on that one!

"Aunt Kristen, I'm cold!" said Johann. Aunt Kristen replied, "Go in the corner, then, it's always ninety degrees."

. . . .

A tomato dad, mom, and son are walking down the street. The tomato son falls behind. The tomato dad walks back to the tomato son, stomps his foot, and yells, "Ketchup!"

. . . .

A man called the local airport. "How long will it take to fly from here to Los Angeles?" he asked. "Um, just a minute," answered the agent. "Wow! That isn't long at all. Thank you!" he said, and hung up.

NEWS ANCHOR: What's the chance of snow today?

WEATHER PERSON: About 50 percent.

NEWS ANCHOR: And what's the chance you're wrong?

WEATHER PERSON: About 50 percent.

On the first day of school, the teacher asked a student, "What are your parents' names?" The student replied, "My father's name is Laughing and my mother's name is Smiling." The teacher said, "Are you kidding?" The student said, "No, Kidding is my brother. I'm Joking!"

LAST TEACHER STANDING

A new teacher was trying to get to know his students. He started class by saying, "Everyone who doesn't think they're smart, stand up." After a few seconds, Haven stood up. The teacher said, "You don't think you're smart, Haven?" Haven said, "I do, sir, but I hate to see you standing there all by yourself."

MAN-EATING CHICKEN

A little boy and his older sister were visiting their grandfather's farm. The older sister decided to play a trick on her younger sibling. She told him that she discovered a man-eating chicken. The brother was frightened and ran inside. Then the sister heard her little brother scream. She ran inside to find her brother screaming at their grandfather, who was eating fried chicken. "What is it?" she asked. The brother turned to her and said, "It's—it's—IT'S A MAN EATING CHICKEN!!!"

A STARRY SURPRISE

Angel and Sammie went camping. They pitched their tent under the stars and went to sleep. Sometime in the middle of the night Angel woke Sammie up and said, "Sammie, look up and tell me what you see." Sammie replied, "I see millions and millions of stars." Angel said, "And what does that mean?" Sammie replied, "There are so many galaxies and unknown places out in space. It's really quite magical!" And Angel said, "Sammie, it means that somebody stole our tent."

DEFINITELY STINKY

A teacher is teaching her class about the word *definitely*. "Can anyone use *definitely* in a sentence?" she asks. Malaura raises her hand and says, "Grass is *definitely* green." "Sometimes grass can be brown," the teacher responds. "Anyone else?" "The sky is *definitely* blue," says Luca. "The sky can be gray if it's cloudy or black at night," the teacher says. Kai raises his hand and says, "Do farts have lumps?" Startled, the teacher says, "No, of course not!" Kai replies, "Then I *definitely* pooped my pants."

THE BOY & THE BARBER

A young boy enters a barbershop and the barber whispers to his customer, "This is the silliest kid in the world. Watch while I prove it to you." The barber puts a dollar bill in one hand and two quarters in the other, then calls the boy over and asks, "Which do you want, son?" The boy takes the quarters and leaves. "What did I tell you?" says the barber. "That kid never learns!" Later, when the customer leaves, he sees the same young boy coming out of the ice cream store. "Hey, son! May I ask you a question? Why did you take the quarters instead of the dollar bill?" The boy licks his cone and replies, "Because the day I take the dollar, the game is over!"

DOUBLE TROUBLE

Mr. and Mrs. Singh have two daughters. One is named Mind Your Own Business and the other is named Trouble. One day the sisters decided to play hide-and-seek. Trouble hid while Mind Your Own Business counted to one hundred. Mind Your Own Business began looking for her sister behind garbage cans and bushes. Then she started looking in and under cars until a police officer approached her and asked, "What are you doing?" "Playing a game," the girl replied. "What is your name?" the officer questioned. "Mind Your Own Business." Furious, the police officer inquired, "Are you looking for trouble?!" The girl replied, "Yes, how did you know?!"

CAT MATH

Santana's teacher said, "If I gave you two cats and another two cats and another two cats, how many cats would you have?" Santana said, "Seven." "No, listen carefully. . . . If I gave you two cats, and another two cats, and another two, how many cats would you have?" "Seven," Santana said again. Santana's teacher sighed. "Let me put it to you differently. If I gave you two apples, and another two apples, and another two, how many apples would you have?" "Six," said Santana. "Good. Now if I gave you two cats, and another two cats, and another two, how many cats would you have?" "Seven!" "Santana, where are you getting seven from?!" "Because I already have a cat!"

A CLEVER WAGER

Tyler says to Naomi, "Let's play a game. I'll ask you a question, and if you don't know the answer, you give me one dollar, but if I don't know the answer to your question, I'll give you ten dollars." Naomi agrees and Tyler asks the first question: "How many continents are in the world?" Naomi shakes her head and hands over one dollar. She then asks Tyler, "What goes up a hill on three legs, but comes down on four?" Tyler thinks about it for a long time, but can't come up with the answer, so he gives ten dollars to Naomi. A little later, a frustrated Tyler says, "So, what does go up a hill on three legs, but comes down on four?" Naomi just shrugs and hands over one dollar.

COLD WATER CLEANING

One morning, Josh's grandpa prepared a breakfast. Josh noticed something on his plate and asked, "Are these plates clean?" His grandpa replied, "They're as clean as cold water can get them." For lunch, Josh was still concerned. "Are you sure these plates are clean?" Without looking up, Grandpa said, "I told you, those dishes are as clean as cold water can get them!" As Josh left, the dog wouldn't let him pass. Grandpa yelled to the dog, "Cold Water, go lie down!"

PET PENGUINS

A woman was driving down the road when a police officer stopped her. The officer looked in the back of the woman's truck and said, "Why are these penguins in your truck?" The woman replied, "These are my penguins. They belong to me." "You need to take them to the zoo," the police officer said. The next day, the officer saw the same woman driving down the road. He pulled her over again. He saw the penguins were still in the truck, but they were wearing sunglasses this time. "I thought I told you to take these penguins to the zoo!" the officer said. "I did," the woman replied. "And today I'm taking them to the beach."

BRAIN FREEZE

An older couple notices they are getting more forgetful. Their doctor tells them to write things down so they'll remember. At home, the wife asks her husband for a bowl of ice cream. "Write it down," she says. The husband says, "No, I can remember that you want a bowl of ice cream." Then she says she wants a bowl of ice cream with whipped cream. "Write it down," she tells him, and again he says, "No, I can remember that you want a bowl of ice cream with whipped cream." Then the wife says she wants a bowl of ice cream with whipped cream and a cherry on top. "Write it down," she tells her husband, and again he says, "No, I got it. You want a bowl of ice cream with whipped cream and a cherry on top." He goes to get the ice cream. After a long time, he comes back and hands his wife a plate of eggs and bacon. The wife stares at the plate for a moment, then looks at her husband and asks, "Where's the toast?"

STILL HIRING

Three teenagers interview for a job at a local coffee shop. The first teenager goes in and has the best interview ever. At the end, the manager says, "By the way, did you notice anything unique about me?"

The first teenager says, "Yeah, you don't have ears!" "I'm sorry," says the manager, "I'm very sensitive about my ears. I'm afraid you aren't the right person for this job."

The second teenager goes in and has the best interview ever. Once again, the manager asks, "Did you notice anything unique about me?" The second teenager says, "I noticed that you don't have any ears." "I'm sorry," says the manager, "I'm very sensitive about my ears. I'm afraid you aren't the right person for this job." As the second teenager is leaving, he says to the third teenager, "Hey, man, whatever you do, don't mention the manager's ears!"

The third teenager has the best interview ever. At the end, the manager says, "Did you notice anything unique about me?" The third teenager looks closely, squints his eyes a bit, and says, "Yeah, you wear contacts, don't you?" "Wow!" says the manager. "I do! How did you know?" "Because," says the third teenager, "there is no way you could wear glasses!"

BONUS
JOKES!

Want a few extra jokes to keep in your back pocket? Here are some classic Q&A jokes to practice out loud and share with your favorite audience.

What does a cloud wear under its raincoat?

Thunderwear!

Why did the turkey cross the road twice?

To show he wasn't a chicken!

What do you call cheese that doesn't belong to you?

Nacho cheese.

How do you know the ocean is friendly?

It waves.

What's a cat's favorite color?

Purrr-ple.

What do you call a sleeping dinosaur?

A dino-snore!

How do you make a tissue dance?

Put a little boogie in it.

How does a penguin build its house?

Igloos it together.

· · · · · · · · · · · · · · · ·

What do you call a hot dog on wheels?

Fast food.

· · · · · · · · · · · · · · · ·

What do you call a bear without any teeth?

A gummy bear.

What did one hat say to the other?

Stay here! I'm going on ahead.

· · · · · · · · · · · · · · · ·

Why did the superhero flush the toilet?

Because it was his doody.

· · · · · · · · · · · · · · · ·

Why did the pie go to the dentist?

It needed a filling.

Where does the chicken like to eat?

At a rooster-ant!

Why did the golfer wear two pairs of pants?

In case he got a hole in one.

What musical instrument is found in the bathroom?

A tuba toothpaste.

What do cats always wear when they go to bed?

Paw-jamas.

Want to hear a pizza joke?

Never mind, it's too cheesy.

How do you make an octopus laugh?

With ten-tickles.

What do you call
a dinosaur with
bad vision?

**A do-you-think-
he-saurus!**

· · · · · · · · · · · · · · · ·

What do you call an
alligator in a vest?

An investi-gator!

· · · · · · · · · · · · · · · ·

Why did the gum
cross the road?

**It was stuck to the
chicken's foot!**

What do you call
a nosy pepper?

Jalapeño business!

· · · · · · · · · · · · · · · ·

Why was the
sand wet?

**Because the
sea weed.**

· · · · · · · · · · · · · · · ·

What do you call
a dinosaur fart?

**A blast from
the past.**

About the Foreword Author

Toby Price is a former teacher and elementary school principal. He is a husband, educator, artist, dad joke connoisseur, and author of *The Almost True Adventures of Tytus the Monkey*. He spends his time advocating for students and kids with special needs. Parents, you can find him as @JediPadmaster on Twitter, where Mr. Price loves connecting, learning, and laughing with other educators and parents. He believes that kids need access to all kinds of books, especially silly ones. He is a father of three beautiful kids, two with autism. He has been married to his lovely wife, Leah, for 21 years. He lives with his family in Mississippi.

· · · · · · · · · · · · · · · · · · · ·

Thank you for coming on this adventure with us! A Brightly Book is expertly designed to provide young readers with a fun, age-appropriate, and hands-on learning experience.

From board books to reads for teens, Brightly helps raise lifelong readers by celebrating the countless adventures and moments of connection that books can offer. We take pride in working with a diverse group of contributors, authors, and partners who provide a multitude of ways to cultivate a love of books and reading in children of all ages.

We hope you and your young readers enjoy this book as much as we do.

Happy reading!

readbrightly.com
Connect with Brightly on all social channels
@readbrightly